W9-CFS-205

Reading/Writing Companion

mheducation.com/prek-12

Send all inquiries to:
McGraw Hill
1325 Avenue of the Americas
New York, NY 10019

ISBN: 978-1-26-573799-3
MHID: 1-26-573799-1

Printed in the United States of America.

5 6 7 8 9 LMN 26 25 24 23 22

A

Welcome to
WONDERS!

We're here to help you set goals to build on the amazing things you already know. We'll also help you reflect on everything you'll learn.

Let's start by taking a look at the incredible things you'll do this year.

You'll build knowledge on exciting topics and find answers to interesting questions.

You'll read fascinating fiction, informational texts, and poetry and respond to what you read with your own thoughts and ideas.

And you'll research and write stories, poems, and essays of your own!

Here's a sneak peek at how you'll do it all.

"Let's go!"

You'll explore new ideas by reading groups of different texts about the same topic. These groups of texts are called *text sets*.

At the beginning of a text set, we'll help you set goals on the My Goals page. You'll see a bar with four boxes beneath each goal. Think about what you already know to fill in the bar. Here's an example.

I can read and understand realistic fiction.

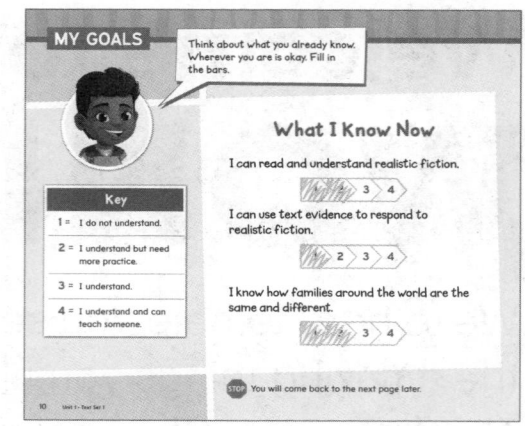

I haven't read realistic fiction before. I'll shade in the **first box**.

I think I can do this, but I want more practice. I'll shade in the first **two boxes**.

I have read and understood realistic fiction, but there are more things I need to know. I'll shade in the first **three boxes**.

I can teach a friend all about realistic fiction. I'll shade in all **four boxes**.

As you move through a text set, you'll explore an essential question and build your knowledge of a topic until you're ready to write about it yourself.

You'll also learn skills that will help you reach your text set goals. At the end of lessons, you'll see a new Check In bar with four boxes.

CHECK IN > 1 > 2 > 3 > 4 >

Reflect on how well you understood a lesson to fill in the bar.

Here are some questions you can ask yourself.

- Was I able to complete the task?

- Was it easy or was it hard?

- Do I think I need more practice?

You have plenty of tools and resources to learn more, such as anchor charts and center activities. You can also reread a lesson or ask a teacher or peer for help.

It's okay if I think I need more practice. The most important thing is that I do my best and keep learning!

Thinking about what works best for me helps me choose what to do next.

At the end of each text set, you'll show off the knowledge you built by completing a fun task. Then you'll return to the second My Goals page where we'll help you reflect on all that you learned.

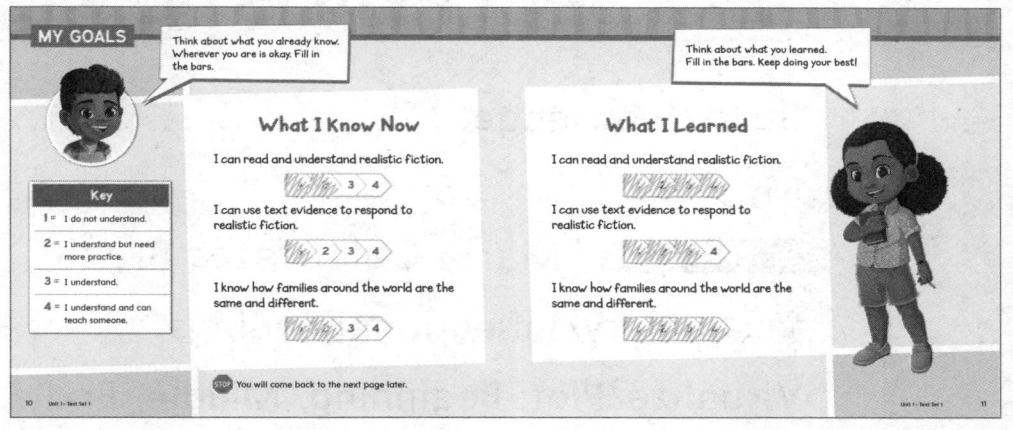

I'll fill in a new set of bars to show how far I've come. I started at 2, but now I'm at 4 because I can read and understand realistic fiction well enough to teach a friend.

I'll follow the same steps as I write my own stories, essays, and poems. I own my learning and you can own yours!

"Let's get started!"

TEXT SET 1 **REALISTIC FICTION**

TEXT SET 2 **FANTASY**

TEXT SET 3 **EXPOSITORY TEXT**

EXTENDED WRITING

CONNECT AND REFLECT

 Digital Tools

Find this eBook and other resources at **my.mheducation.com**.

Build Knowledge

How are families around the world the same and different?

Build Vocabulary

Write new words you learned about families around the world. Draw lines and circles for the words you write.

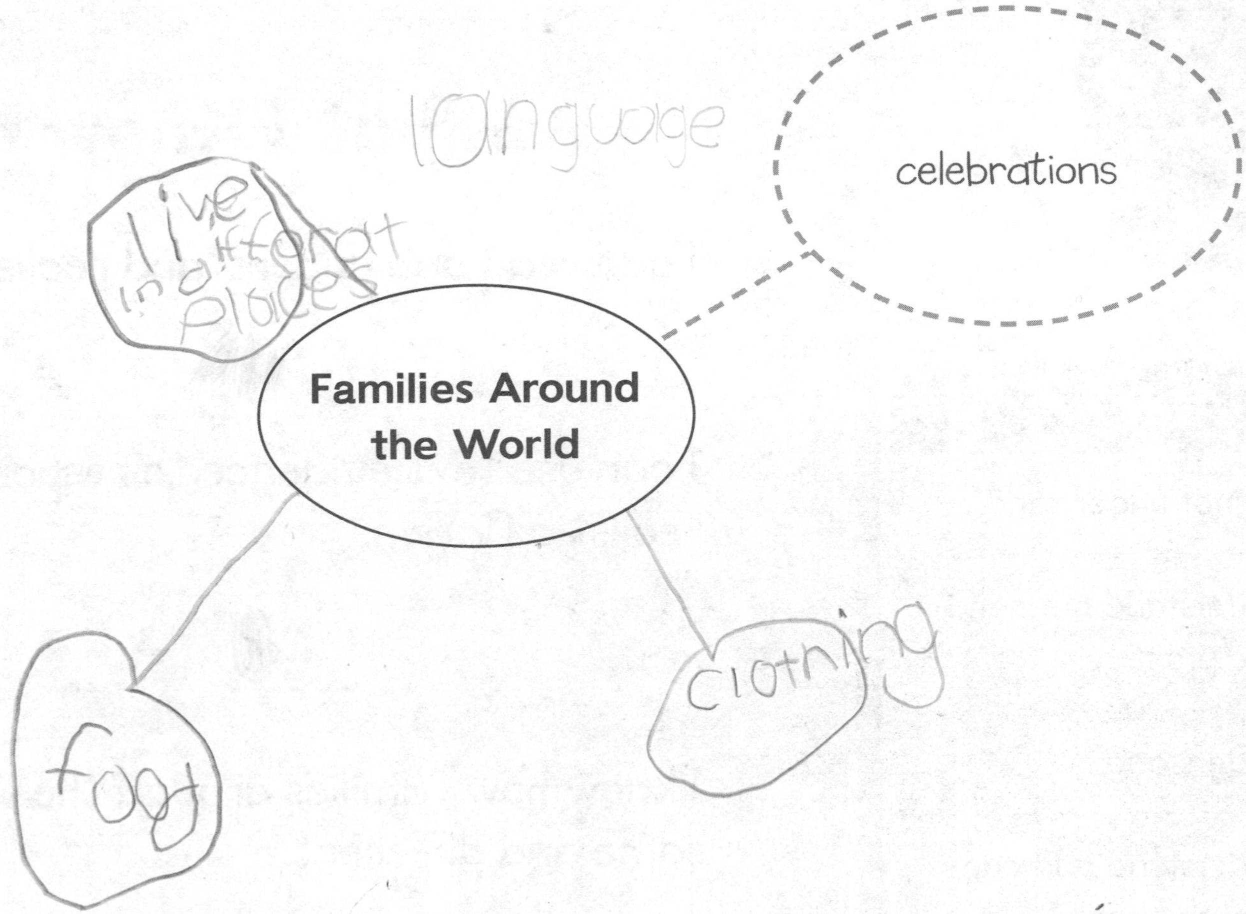

language

celebrations

live in different places

Families Around the World

food

clothing

Go online to **my.mheducation.com** and read the "Family Photos" Blast. Think about how families around the world spend time together. Then blast back your response.

MY GOALS

Think about what you already know. Wherever you are is okay. Fill in the bars.

What I Know Now

I can read and understand realistic fiction.

I can use text evidence to respond to realistic fiction.

I know how families around the world are the same and different.

| 1 | 2 | 3 | 4 |

STOP You will come back to the next page later.

Key

1 =	I do not understand.
2 =	I understand but need more practice.
3 =	I understand.
4 =	I understand and can teach someone.

Think about what you learned.
Fill in the bars. Keep doing your best!

What I Learned

I can read and understand realistic fiction.

1 > 2 > 3 > 4

I can use text evidence to respond to realistic fiction.

1 > 2 > 3 > 4

I know how families around the world are the same and different.

1 > 2 > 3 > 4

My Goal I can read and understand realistic fiction.

TAKE NOTES

As you read, write down interesting words and important events.

_____

_____

_____

_____

_____

_____

_____

_____

_____

Maria Celebrates Brazil

Essential Question

? **How are families around the world the same and different?**

Read about a family from Brazil.

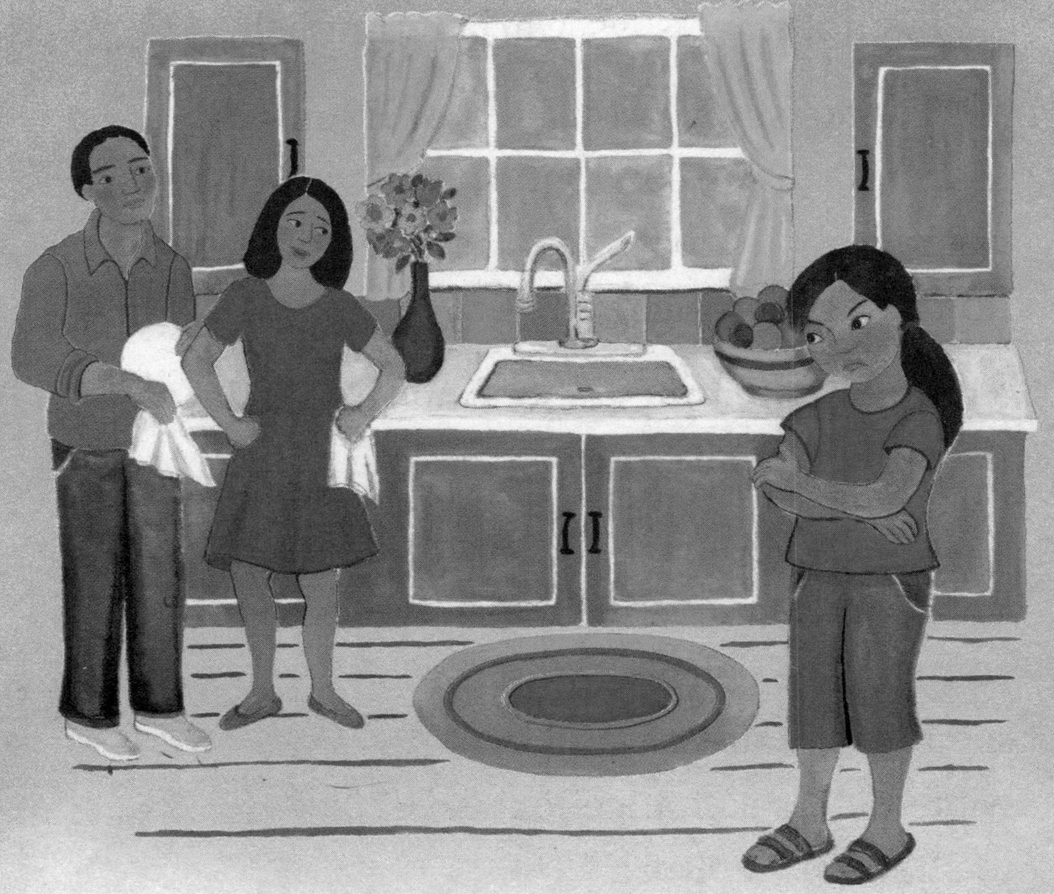

Maria and her family are in their bright, hot kitchen. "Please, Mãe, por favor!" Maria begs.

Mãe speaks Portuguese. This is the **language** of Brazil. "No matter how much you beg or **plead**, you must go to practice. The parade is next week."

FIND TEXT EVIDENCE 🔍

Read

Paragraph 1

Character, Setting, Events

Draw a box around the characters. Where are they?

They are in the kichen.

Paragraph 2

Plot: Beginning, Middle, End

Circle what Maria's parents want her to do in the beginning of the story.

Reread

Author's Craft

Why does the author use Portuguese words in the story?

Read

Paragraphs 1–3

Plot: Beginning, Middle, End

Circle what Maria says about going to practice. **Draw a box** around the reason she feels this way.

Paragraph 4

Visualize

Underline details that help you picture the parade. What can the family share there?

They Share
food Clothing
and theineculture

Reread

Author's Craft

How does the author use dialogue to show the way each character feels?

"It's not **fair**," says Maria in English.

Mãe does not know a lot of English. Maria is surprised when she asks, "What is not fair about going to practice? You must do the right thing."

"Ana **invited** me to her house," Maria answers. "I want to go!"

Pai says, "Maria, the parade is important. People from around the world come to see it. They try our food, see how we dress and how we live. It is a chance for us to **share** our **culture**."

"I know but I really want to see Ana," says Maria.

Pai says, "Maria, you can see Ana another time. They are giving out costumes at practice today."

Maria thinks about her father's words. Pai is right. She and the other children have worked hard for a year. They practiced their dance steps over and over. They even made their own bright, colorful costumes.

Janet Broxon

FIND TEXT EVIDENCE

`Read`

Paragraphs 1–2

Character, Setting, Events

Draw a box around what Maria can do another time. What important event is happening today?

They are
getting their
costumes.

Paragraph 3

Inflectional Endings

Circle the ending added to *practice*. **Underline** what the children did over and over to do it better.

`Reread`

Author's Craft

Why does the author describe Maria's thoughts?

Read

Paragraph 1

Plot: Beginning, Middle, End

How does Maria feel about going to practice now?

she wants to go

Paragraph 2

Character, Setting, Events

Underline the two sentences that tell when and where the parade takes place.

Reread

Author's Craft

Why does the author use an illustration to support details about the setting?

"You're right," Maria says to her father. "I'll go to practice. I'll tell Ana I cannot visit her."

One week passes. Lots of people line the streets. The children in Maria's group are wearing their sparkling costumes. They know each dance step. They dance to the beat.

The crowd moves **aside** as they make their way down the street.

When the crowd moves away, Maria sees a woman with a camera. She is hurrying. The woman **scurries** by Maria. She puts her camera to her eye. Maria smiles from ear to ear. She is excited to be in the parade. Click! The woman takes a picture of Maria. Maria is proud of her hard work!

Janet Broxon

Retell

Use your notes and think about what happens in "Maria Celebrates Brazil." Then retell the events in the order that they happen.

FIND TEXT EVIDENCE 🔍

Read
Paragraph 2
Visualize
Circle the person Maria sees when the crowd moves away. **Underline** details that help you picture what the character is doing.

Plot: Beginning, Middle, End
How does Maria feel about going to practice at the end of the story?

proud

Vocabulary

Talk with a partner about each word. Then answer the questions.

aside

Mia moved **aside** to let her brother pass.

Why do you move aside on a sidewalk?

_____

_____

culture

A parade in February is part of the **culture** of Brazil.

What is an important event in your culture?

_____

_____

> **Build Your Word List** In your reader's notebook, write a definition for an interesting word from the story. Use a dictionary to help you.

fair

We are **fair** and treat everyone the same.

What is one way to be fair at school?

_____

_____

invited

We **invited** the school to watch our play.

Tell about an event you were invited to.

_____

_____

language

My friend speaks more than one **language**.

What language do you want to learn?

_____

_____

plead

My little brother will **plead** with me to play with him.

What is something you might plead for?

_____

_____

scurries

The squirrel **scurries** up the tree.

What other animal scurries in nature?

_____

_____

share

I will **share** my orange with my friend.

What is something you can share with a friend?

_____

_____

Inflectional Endings

To understand the meaning of a word, you can separate a base word from the ending, such as -ed or -ing.

🔍 **FIND TEXT EVIDENCE**

I'm not sure what hurrying _means._ Hurry means "to move quickly." The ending -ing _can mean "something happening right now." I think_ hurrying _means "moving quickly right now."_

Maria sees a woman with a camera. She is hurrying.

Your Turn Use the ending to figure out the meaning of the word below in "Maria Celebrates Brazil."

wearing, page 16 _____

_____

CHECK IN ▷ 1 ⟩ 2 ⟩ 3 ⟩ 4 ⟩

Janet Broxon

Visualize

When you visualize, you use the author's words to form pictures in your mind about a story.

🔍 **FIND TEXT EVIDENCE**

When you read the last sentence on page 15, use the author's words to help you visualize the costumes.

Page 15

Maria thinks about her father's words. Pai is right. She and the other children have worked hard for a year. They practiced their dance steps over and over. They even made their own bright, colorful costumes.

I reread, "They even made their own bright, colorful costumes." I can picture in my mind the bright colors of the costumes. This helps me visualize what their costumes are like.

Quick Tip

To help you visualize, pay attention to words that tell about actions, or what people do. Words that describe the way something looks or sounds will also help you.

Your Turn Reread the second paragraph on page 16. What details help you picture the parade and Maria's group of dancers?

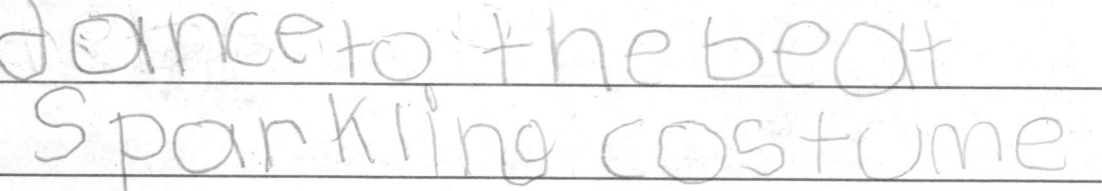

dance to the beat
Sparkling costume

CHECK IN 1 2 3 4

Plot: Beginning, Middle, End

"Maria Celebrates Brazil" is realistic fiction. It is a made-up story that could really happen. A character is a person in the story. A character's feelings can change in the beginning, middle, and end of a story.

FIND TEXT EVIDENCE

The characters in "Maria Celebrates Brazil" act like real people. I can tell how a character's feelings change in different parts of this realistic fiction story.

Page 14

"It's not **fair**," says Maria in English.

Mãe does not know a lot of English. Maria is surprised when she asks, "What is not fair about going to practice? You must do the right thing."

"Ana **invited** me to her house," Maria answers. "I want to go!"

Pai says, "Maria, the parade is important. People from around the world come to see it. They try our food, see how we dress, and how we live. It is a chance for us to **share** our **culture**."

Beginning, Middle, End

In the beginning of the story, Maria wants to skip practice and go to a friend's house. Her parents remind her why practice is important.

Your Turn How do Maria's feelings about going to practice change in different parts of the story?

In the beginning she didn't want to go but at the end she was happy

CHECK IN 1 2 3 4

Janet Broxon

Character, Setting, Events

Characters are important people or animals in a story. The setting tells when and where a story takes place. The events are what happens.

FIND TEXT EVIDENCE

As I read pages 13 and 14 of "Maria Celebrates Brazil," I learn who the characters are, where the story begins, and what the characters are doing.

Quick Tip

Think about what the characters do and say. Identify their feelings from words in the text and illustrations. Use these details about the characters to help you describe each event.

Character	Setting	Events
Maria Mãe Pai	The family's kitchen one week before the parade	Maria tells her parents she wants to miss dance practice. Her parents want her to go to practice.

Your Turn Continue rereading the story. Identify the characters and describe the settings and events to complete the graphic organizer.

CHECK IN 1 2 3 4

Character	Setting	Events
Maria Mãe Pai	The family's kitchen one week before the parade	Maria tells her parents she wants to miss dance practice. Her parents want her to go to practice.

I can use text evidence to respond to realistic fiction.

Respond to Reading

COLLABORATE

Talk about the prompt below. Use your notes and text evidence to support your response.

How do Maria's parents help her to make a good decision and do the right thing?

_____

_____

_____

_____

_____

_____

Quick Tip

Use these sentence starters to help you organize your text evidence.

At the beginning of the story, Maria...

Maria's father...

At the end, Maria...

Grammar Connections

Begin the first word of each sentence with a capital letter. Use a period at the end of each sentence to show the end of a statement.

CHECK IN 1 > 2 > 3 > 4

Food from Other Countries

COLLABORATE

Create a poster about a food or dish that was brought to the United States by people from another country. With a partner, follow the research process.

Step 1 **Set a Goal** Decide on a topic for your poster.

Write your topic: _____

Step 2 **Identify Sources** Keywords will help you find sources of information for your poster. Keywords are important words you use when talking or writing about your topic. Discuss keywords to use.

Write two keywords: _____

Step 3 **Find and Record Information** Find information in your sources and take notes. Write down each source you used in your research.

Step 4 **Organize and Combine Information** Group together facts that tell about the same ideas, such as where the food came from, who brought it to the United States, or how it is prepared.

Step 5 **Create and Present** Add pictures and captions to your poster. As a class, display and discuss the different foods from around the world.

Quick Tip

Think about research questions for your poster. Ask what you want to learn. These questions will help you figure out the keywords to use in your Internet searches.

When you do Internet research, keywords tell the search engine what to look for.

CHECK IN ⟩ 1 ⟩ 2 ⟩ 3 ⟩ 4 ⟩

Big Red Lollipop

? How does the author show the way Rubina feels when Sana and Ami do not understand her problem?

Talk About It Look at the illustration on page 12. Talk with a partner about how you think Rubina feels.

Cite Text Evidence Write clues from the text and the illustration where the author shows Rubina's feelings.

Literature Anthology:
pages 10–30

💡 **Combine Information**

Look back at page 11. Why is going to a birthday party important to Rubina? Use text evidence to support your response.

Clues from the Text	Clues from the Illustration
They'll laugh at me!	She's frowning and looking away

Rubina's Feelings

frustated sad worried mad

Write The author shows Rubina is feeling ___mad___ the feeling worried the frustated

CHECK IN 1 > 2 > 3 > 4 >

? **How does the author use an illustration to help you understand the way Rubina feels toward Sana in the middle of the story?**

Talk About It Look at the illustration on pages 20–21 of the **Literature Anthology**. Talk about what it shows.

Cite Text Evidence What clues from the text and the illustration help you understand how Rubina feels?

Clues from the Text	Clues from the Illustration
She was screaming im goIng	She was chasing her sister around the house.

Write The text and illustration help me understand that

_____

_____

_____

Quick Tip

As you read, use these sentence starters to talk about how Rubina feels.

Rubina compares her sister to...

Rubina's face looks...

Make Inferences

An inference is an idea you have from clues in the story's text and illustrations. Make an inference that answers the question: Why does Rubina use the word "rat" to describe how quickly Sana moves?

CHECK IN 1 2 3 4

? How does the author help you understand the character Rubina?

Talk About It Reread page 28. Talk with a partner about what Rubina thinks and does.

Cite Text Evidence Complete the chart with what Rubina thinks and what she does when her sister is invited to a party.

What Rubina Thinks	What Rubina Does
Rubina thinks shouldn't want to go to the party.	She takes care of maryam so sand can to the party by herself.

Write The author helps me understand that Rubina is

hipefefo

CHECK IN 1 2 3 4

Respond to Reading

COLLABORATE

Discuss the prompt below. Use your notes and text evidence to support your response.

Why does Sana bring Rubina a lollipop at the end of the story?

_____

_____

_____

_____

_____

_____

_____

_____

Quick Tip

Use these sentence starters to organize your text evidence.

Sana feels...
Sana remembers...
Sana wants to...

CHECK IN 1 2 3 4

A Look at Families

Families around the world do some things the same. They have differences, too. Let's take a look at how families in different cultures live.

Families live in different places. Some families live in large cities. They might live in tall apartment buildings. Many families live in the same building.

Literature Anthology: pages 32–35

Reread the first paragraph. **Underline** two sentences about families around the world. What will you look at as the text continues?

_____

_____

Reread paragraph 2. **Circle** details that tell about where some families live.

COLLABORATE

Talk with a partner about how people in large cities may live. Use the details in the text and the photograph to support your ideas.

Some families live near water. Some families live in houses on stilts. Stilts are tall poles. They keep the homes safe from water.

Reread the paragraph. **Draw a box** around the author's definition of stilts. Look for the stilts in the photograph.

Why do some families live in houses on stilts? **Underline** the text evidence. Write your answer here.

_____

_____

_____

COLLABORATE

Ask and answer questions about the different kinds of homes people live in around the world. Support your ideas with details from pages 30–31.

? **Why does the author tell about families from many parts of the world?**

Talk About It Reread pages 32–35 of the **Literature Anthology**. What does the author tell us about families?

Cite Text Evidence Write details from the text that show how all families are the same.

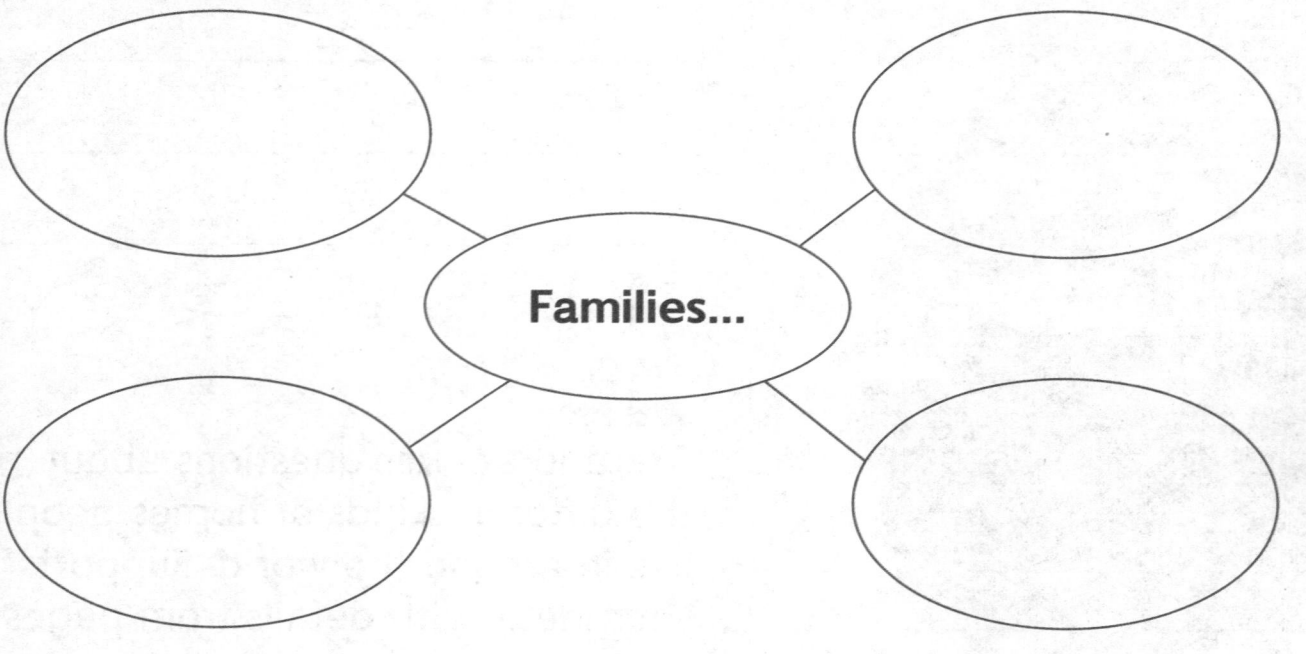

Families...

Write The author wants to explain that _____

_____

_____

Lone Oatey/blue jean images/Getty Images

CHECK IN ⟩ 1 ⟩ 2 ⟩ 3 ⟩ 4

Captions

Captions are words that tell about a photo, map, or other text feature. Authors use captions to give information about what appears in the text feature.

FIND TEXT EVIDENCE
Look back at the photographs and captions on page 32 in the **Literature Anthology**. What did you learn from the captions?

_____

_____

_____

Your Turn Look back at the photos and captions on page 33. How do the captions help you to understand the purpose of these photographs?

_____

_____

_____

Quick Tip

Authors use photographs and captions in expository text to help you to understand the topic. Authors often use captions to point out an important detail shown in a photograph.

CHECK IN ▷ 1 ❭ 2 ❭ 3 ❭ 4

COLLABORATE

? **What have you learned from the selections and song about friends and families doing things together?**

Talk About It Read the song. Talk about what the song says about being with friends. How is this like being with family?

Cite Text Evidence Circle a clue from the song that tells you how friends are like family.

Write This song and the selections I read help me

understand that _____

_____

_____

_____

_____

_____

_____

The More We Get Together

The more we get together, together, together

The more we get together, the happier we'll be.

For your friends are my friends, and my friends are your friends,

The more we get together, the happier we'll be.

— German Folk Song

CHECK IN 1 2 3 4

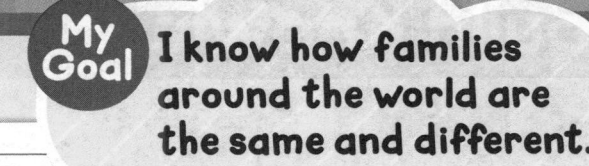

My Goal I know how families around the world are the same and different.

Write a Journal Entry

Think about the children and their families in the stories you read. How do these characters help you understand how families are the same and different?

1. Look at your Build Knowledge notes in your reader's notebook.

2. Write a journal entry about what you learned about the families from different cultures. Explain what all the families have in common.

3. Include some of the new words you learned. Use text evidence to support your ideas about families from around the world. Be sure to use examples from three of the stories you read.

Think about what you learned in this text set. Fill in the bars on page 11.

Build Knowledge

Build Vocabulary

Write new words you learned about friends helping friends. Draw lines and circles for the words you write.

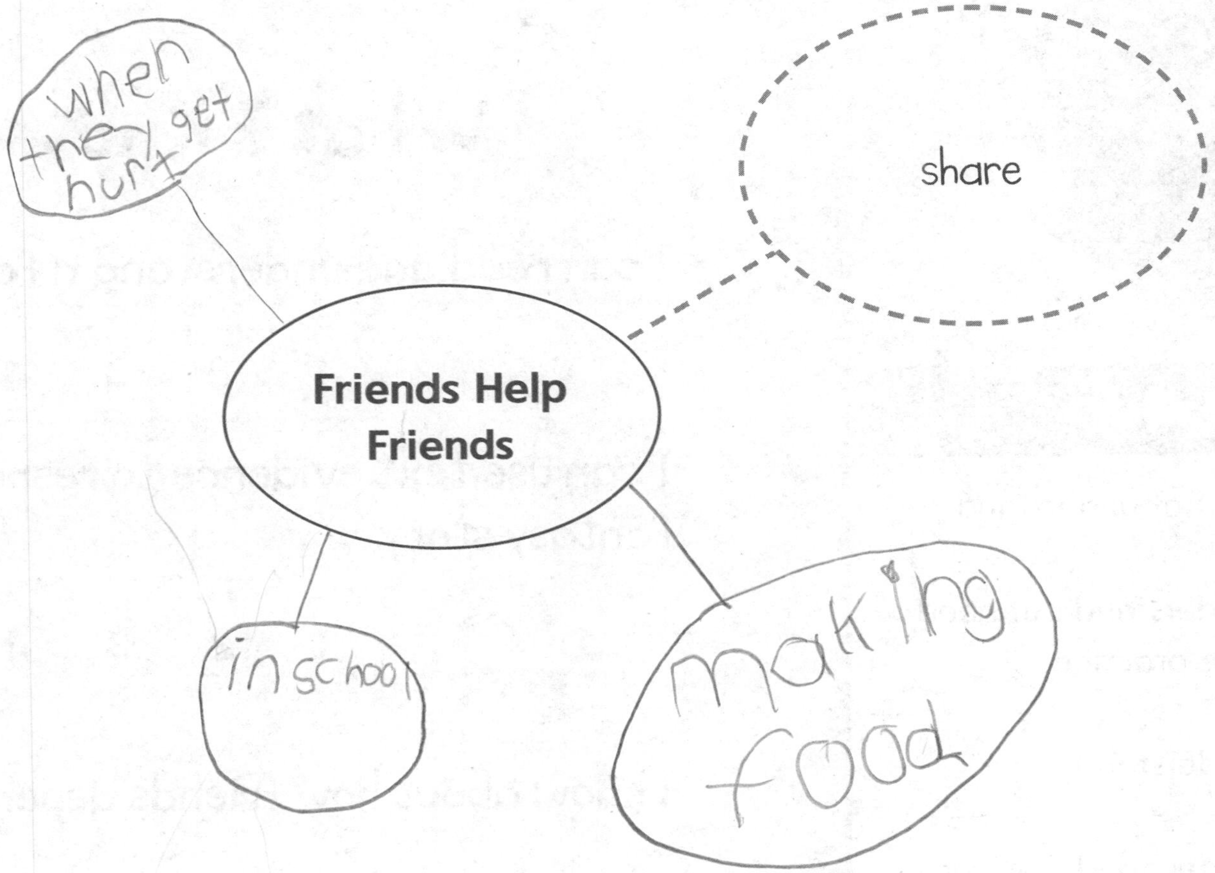

when they get hurt

share

Friends Help Friends

in school

makIng food

Go online to **my.mheducation.com** and read the "We Celebrate Our Friends" Blast. Think about how friends show they care about their friends. Then blast back your response.

Think about what you already know. Fill in the bars. There are no wrong answers here.

Key

1 = I do not understand.

2 = I understand but need more practice.

3 = I understand.

4 = I understand and can teach someone.

What I Know Now

I can read and understand a fantasy story.

| 1 | 2 | 3 | 4 |

I can use text evidence to respond to a fantasy story.

| 1 | 2 | 3 | 4 |

I know about how friends depend on each other.

| 1 | 2 | 3 | 4 |

 You will come back to the next page later.

Think about what you learned. Fill in the bars. What helped you the most?

What I Learned

I can read and understand a fantasy story.

1 2 3 4

I can use text evidence to respond to a fantasy story.

1 2 3 4

I know about how friends depend on each other.

1 2 3 4

SHARED READD

My Goal I can read and understand a fantasy story.

TAKE NOTES

As you read, write down interesting words and important events.

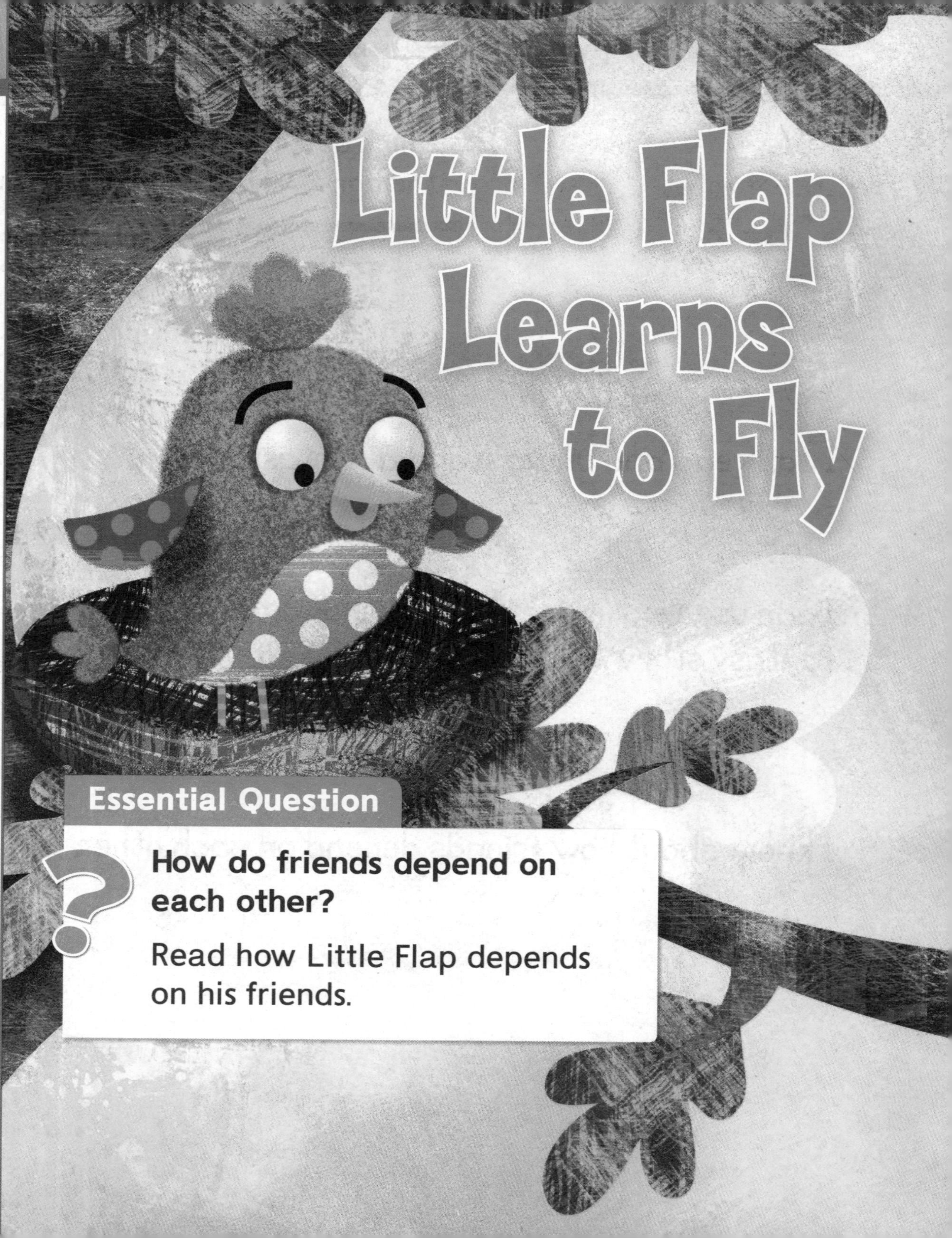

Little Flap Learns to Fly

Essential Question

How do friends depend on each other?

Read how Little Flap depends on his friends.

Little Flap was happy living in his nest. His friends, Fluff and Tuff, lived in the nest next to him. Every morning they sang songs together. Their parents brought them worms to eat.

One day Fluff asked, "Can we get our own worms?"

Tuff said, "We can if we learn to fly."

Fluff said, "Yes! Let's learn to fly."

Tim Beaumont

FIND TEXT EVIDENCE

Read

Paragraph 1

Visualize

Draw a box around details that help you visualize why Little Flap is happy living in his nest.

Paragraphs 2–4

Theme

Underline what Fluff wants to get. What must the little birds do first?

learn to fly

Reread

Author's Craft

How does the author use dialogue to show what the little birds want to do?

FIND TEXT EVIDENCE

Read

Illustrations

Where is Little Flap, and why does he look scared in the illustration?

_____

_____

Paragraphs 2–3

Theme

Circle why Fluff wants the birds to practice flapping their wings. What do Tuff and Little Flap do?

copied Fluff's
actions.

Reread

Author's Craft

What details help you understand the way Little Flap feels?

Little Flap **peered** over the edge of his nest. It was very high up. When he looked down, the ground seemed very far away. He felt scared! He was too **afraid** to tell his friends about his fear so he kept his feelings a **secret**.

Fluff said, "Let's practice flapping our wings. It will make them strong. Watch."

Tuff and Little Flap watched Fluff. Then they copied her **actions**.

Soon it was time to fly. Little Flap could no longer keep his feelings a secret. He asked, "Will I fall? I don't want to get hurt."

Tuff said, "You can **depend** on Fluff and me. We're your friends."

Fluff said, "I have an idea. We will go first and show you how. Then you can try. If you fall, Tuff and I will **rescue** you."

Tuff said, "Yes, we can save you!" Tuff and Fluff jumped out of the nest. They flew!

Little Flap looked down **nervously**. He still felt uneasy, but he felt braver with his friends. "Okay," he said. "Let's try!"

Tim Beaumont

FIND TEXT EVIDENCE

Paragraph 1
Base Words

Find the word *asked*. **Circle** the word without the ending *-ed*. **Circle** the question Little Flap asks.

Paragraphs 2–4
Theme

Underline Fluff's idea. How can Little Flap depend on his friends?

help him learn to fly and rescue him.

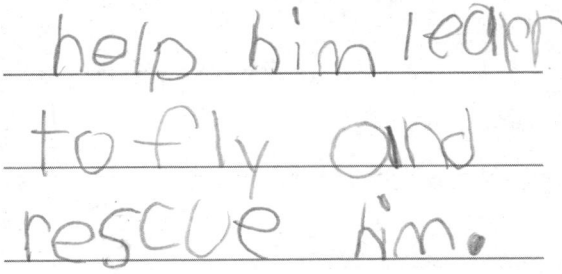

Reread
Author's Craft

How does the author use dialogue to show the birds are good friends?

FIND TEXT EVIDENCE

Read

Paragraph 1

Visualize

Underline words that help you visualize the actions the birds do together.

Paragraphs 2–3

Theme

Circle what Fluff and Tuff tell Little Flap. Why do they say these things?

to show
their support

Reread

Author's Craft

How does the author show Fluff and Tuff's excitement?

The three birds stood together on the branch. They counted, "One! Two! Three!" Then they flapped their wings fast and jumped. Little Flap lifted into the air.

"You're flying just right!" said Fluff.

"You're flying **perfectly!**" said Tuff.

All three little birds landed in a patch of soft, green grass.

Little Flap said, "Now I know I can always depend on you, Fluff and Tuff! You are my friends."

Then he found a big, juicy worm and shared it with his friends.

Now Little Flap likes flying!

Retell

Use your notes and think about the characters, setting, and events in "Little Flap Learns to Fly." Retell the most important details in the order that they happen in the story.

FIND TEXT EVIDENCE

Read

Paragraphs 1–2

Theme

Underline the sentence that describes the birds' safe landing. **Circle** what Little Flap then says.

Paragraph 3

Make Inferences

How does the author show that Little Flap is a good friend to Fluff and Tuff?

_____

_____

_____

_____

_____

_____

Vocabulary

**Talk with a partner about each word.
Then answer the questions.**

actions

The girl's **actions** helped her team win.

What actions help you do well in school?

_____

_____

afraid

Our dog is **afraid** of thunder.

What is something you are afraid of?

_____

_____

> ✏️ **Build Your Word List** Choose an interesting word that you noted. Look up the word's meaning and pronunciation using a dictionary online.

depend

Nick and Maria **depend** on Dad to help them learn to ride a bike.

How do you depend on family members?

_____

_____

nervously

Maya waited **nervously** for her running race to begin.

What did you wait nervously to do?

_____

_____

peered

The dog **peered** through the hole in the fence.

What did you see when you peered out the classroom window?

_____

_____

perfectly

The ball is **perfectly** round.

What is something that is perfectly flat?

_____

_____

rescue

We saw the boy **rescue** the cat from the tree.

What is another word for *rescue*?

_____

_____

secret

Mandy whispered a **secret** to me.

What is special about a secret?

_____

_____

Base Words

To understand the meaning of a word, try to separate the base word from an ending, such as *-ed* or *–ing*.

FIND TEXT EVIDENCE

I'm not sure what landed *means.* Land *can mean "to move down onto the ground." The ending* –ed *means this action happened in the past. So,* landed *means "moved down onto the ground."*

All three little birds landed in a patch of soft, green grass.

Your Turn Use the base word to figure out the meaning of a word in the story.

jumped, page 43 _____

_____

CHECK IN 1 2 3 4

Visualize

When you visualize, you form pictures in your mind about the characters, setting, and events in the story.

🔍 **FIND TEXT EVIDENCE**

After reading page 42 of "Little Flap Learns to Fly," I know Little Flap is thinking about flying. What words does the author use to help readers visualize the nest?

Page 42

> Little Flap peered over the edge of his nest. It was very high up. When he looked down, the ground seemed very far away.

I read that the nest "was very high up" and the ground "seemed very far away." From these details, I can visualize the nest.

Quick Tip

Pay attention to words that tell how something looks, feels, or sounds. This will help you visualize the story.

Your Turn Reread page 45. What words help you visualize where the birds land?

_____

_____

_____

CHECK IN ⟩ 1 ⟩ 2 ⟩ 3 ⟩ 4 ⟩

Illustrations

"Little Flap Learns to Fly" is a fantasy story with made-up characters who could not be real. Often illustrations help show the setting of a fantasy story and how animal characters behave, or act, like real people.

🔍 FIND TEXT EVIDENCE

In this fantasy story, I can use illustrations to help me describe the setting and how the animal characters act.

Page 40

Little Flap Learns to Fly

Essential Question

How do friends depend on each other?

Read how Little Flap depends on his friends.

Illustrations

In this illustration, Little Flap is in his nest. His face looks happy when he looks over at his friends. I know birds do not have friends.

Your Turn Describe an illustration that helps show how the characters act like friends do in real life.

COLLABORATE

_____

_____

_____

CHECK IN ⟩ 1 ⟩ 2 ⟩ 3 ⟩ 4 ⟩

Theme

Quick Tip

Illustrations can help you understand details in a text. They can also show details in the story that are not in the text.

The theme of a story is the message, or big idea, that the author wants to tell readers. To figure out the theme, think about what the characters say and do.

FIND TEXT EVIDENCE

As I read page 42 of "Little Flap Learns to Fly," I learn that Little Flap is afraid to fly. I think this is a clue to the story's theme.

> **Clue**
> Little Flap is afraid to fly.

Your Turn Continue reading the story. Fill in additional clues and the theme in the graphic organizer.

CHECK IN ❯ 1 ❯ 2 ❯ 3 ❯ 4 ❯

Clue

Little Flap is afraid to fly.

Clue

Little Flaps friends help him learn to fly

Clue

They shared a worm and learned to fly

Theme

Frieds can help each other learn

My Goal I can use text evidence to respond to a fantasy story.

Respond to Reading

COLLABORATE

Talk about the prompt below. Use your notes and text evidence to support your response.

Why does Little Flap share the worm with his friends at the end?

_____

_____

_____

_____

_____

_____

_____

_____

Quick Tip

Use these sentence starters to help you organize your text evidence.

Little Flap tells...

He wants to...

The friends know...

Grammar Connections

Use *a* before nouns that start with a consonant. Use *an* before nouns that start with a vowel.

a bird
an eagle

CHECK IN 1 2 3 4

We Depend on Friends

With a partner, create a list of ways we depend on our friends. Follow the research process to create your list.

Step 1 **Set a Goal** You want to find out about the times we depend on friends. Decide on questions you will ask. Write examples of questions here:

_____

_____

Step 2 **Identify Sources** In a small group, ask and answer each other's questions.

Step 3 **Find and Record Information** Take notes on your classmates' answers. Be sure to write down their names and responses.

Step 4 **Organize and Combine Information** Plan how to show the responses in a clear and interesting way.

Step 5 **Create and Present** Print and illustrate the list. Take turns presenting your work. Be sure to use a tone of voice that shows how each response is important.

> **Quick Tip**
>
> You can tell information about a time a friend helped you to solve a problem, learn something new, or just feel better about something.

CHECK IN 1 > 2 > 3 > 4

Help! A Story of Friendship

? **What does the dialogue at the beginning of the story tell you about Mouse and Hedgehog?**

Literature Anthology: pages 36–57

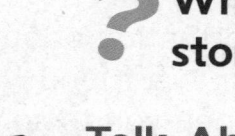
COLLABORATE

Talk About It Reread pages 37–38. Discuss the dialogue, or what Mouse and Hedgehog talk about.

Cite Text Evidence Write about what the two characters say about Snake.

Mouse Says	Hedgehog Says
snake are dangerous to mice	Snake woud never hurt you

Write The dialogue helps me understand _____

_____

Quick Tip

Text evidence is an example from a text. It can be words or phrases used to answer questions about the text. Use text evidence to support your ideas.

Make Inferences

An inference is an idea based on clues in the story's details. Do you think Hedgehog and Snake are good friends? Use text evidence to explain your answer.

CHECK IN 〉 1 〉 2 〉 3 〉 4

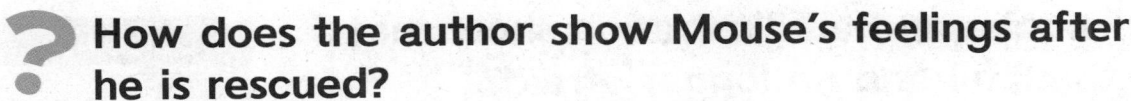

? **How does the author show Mouse's feelings after he is rescued?**

Talk About It Reread page 51 of the **LIterature Anthology.** Talk about what Mouse says and does.

Cite Text Evidence What details on page 51 tell you the way Mouse feels? Write the text evidence.

Detail 1	Detail 2
Mouse turned a jeep shade of Pink.	Because I would never hunt you.

Write I know the way Mouse feels because _____

_____

_____

Quick Tip

As you read, use these sentence starters to talk about how Mouse feels.

Mouse looks...

Mouse says...

Combine Information

Details you already read will help you understand events in the story. Why is Mouse surprised that Snake has saved him? Use details from pages 48–50 to explain your answer.

CHECK IN 1 2 3 4

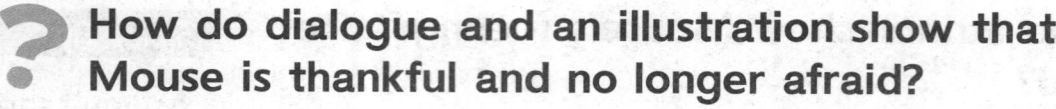

? **How do dialogue and an illustration show that Mouse is thankful and no longer afraid?**

Quick Tip

Details that tell what Mouse does or show how he looks can help you understand his feelings.

COLLABORATE

Talk About It Reread pages 54 and 55 of the **Literature Anthology**. Talk about what Mouse says on page 54. Discuss what the illustration shows on page 55.

Cite Text Evidence Fill in the chart with details that help you understand how Mouse feels.

Detail	Detail	Detail

Write I know Mouse is thankful and no longer afraid

because he _____

_____

_____

CHECK IN 1 ⟩ 2 ⟩ 3 ⟩ 4 ⟩

My Goal — I can use text evidence to respond to a fantasy story.

Respond to Reading

COLLABORATE

Discuss the prompt below. Use your notes and text evidence to support your response.

What does Mouse learn about listening to gossip?

_____

_____

_____

_____

_____

_____

_____

_____

CHECK IN 1 2 3 4

The Enormous Turnip

Other people in their village saw (the family) tugging at the turnip. "Let us help you!" they cried. "Many hands make light work."

The villagers had an idea. They held on to each other's waists to make a chain. Together, they all pulled at the turnip in the ground. Finally, the ground rumbled, and the turnip popped out!

Literature Anthology: pages 58–59

Reread paragraph 1. **Circle** what the villagers see. What do they do next?

They help Them.

Reread paragraph 2. How do the neighbors pull out the turnip? **Underline** text evidence to answer.

COLLABORATE

Talk with a partner about how the last sentence helps show that the turnip is enormous.

Alison Jay

The farmer chopped up the turnip. His wife got a big pot. "Turnip soup for all who helped!" he announced.

All the neighbors took a serving. "We all worked together to find a solution to the problem," said the farmer. "So now we all get a tasty meal as a reward."

Reread paragraph 1. **Underline** what the farmer and his wife do with the turnip. Who are they making turnip soup for?

The people who helped them

Reread paragraph 2. **Circle** what the farmer says about working together.

COLLABORATE

Discuss how the author uses dialogue to explain why the farmer and his wife share the soup.

? What do the villagers mean when they say, "Many hands make light work"?

 **Talk About It** Reread pages 58 and 59 of the **Literature Anthology**. Discuss how the family depends on neighbors to help solve the problem in the folktale.

Cite Text Evidence Fill in the chart with text evidence that shows how "many hands make light work."

Page	Text Evidence
58	thay held tern each waists
59	the nabrs see them.
59	The thay soy the padn

Write "Many hands make light work" means _____

_____

Alison Jay

Evaluate Information

Do you agree that "many hands make light work"? Think about your own experiences. Can you think of a time this saying was true? Can you think of a time it was not true?

CHECK IN   1   2   3   4

Character

Authors often use what the characters do and say to help show the theme in a folktale. A folktale's theme is the big idea that the author wants to tell readers.

FIND TEXT EVIDENCE

The author uses what the villagers say on page 59 to show why they want to help. The dialogue shows the theme about why people should work together.

> "Let us help you!" they cried. "Many hands make light work."

Your Turn Talk about what the farmer says in the last paragraph on page 59. How does the author use the farmer's words to show why people should work together?

_____

_____

_____

_____

Quick Tip

The narrator of "The Enormous Turnip" does not tell the theme. But the author shows that working together is important from the actions and dialogue of the characters.

CHECK IN 1 2 3 4

MAKE CONNECTIONS

? **What have you learned from the selections and the painting about the different ways friends depend on each other?**

Talk About It Look at the painting. Talk about what the girls are doing. Discuss different ways they may depend on each other.

Cite Text Evidence Circle the clues from the painting and caption that show what the girls are doing together.

Write The selections I read and the painting all show

_____

_____

_____

_____

_____

_____

This painting is called _Breton Girls Dancing, Pont-Aven,_ by Paul Gauguin.

Quick Tip
Use these sentence starters to describe what the girls are doing and how they feel.

The girls are...

The girls look...

They help each other...

CHECK IN 1 > 2 > 3 > 4 >

SHOW YOUR KNOWLEDGE

Give an Award

Think about the friends in the stories you read. Think about how the characters help and are kind. How is someone you know like these characters? Give this person an award for being a dependable person.

1. Look at your Build Knowledge notes in your reader's notebook.

2. Write your reasons why someone you know is like the friends from three different stories. Write about why this person is dependable and deserves the award.

3. Include some of the new words you learned. Remember to use evidence from three stories to support your ideas.

Think about what you learned in this text set. Fill in the bars on page 39.

Build Knowledge

Essential Question

What happens when families work together?

Build Vocabulary

Write new words you learned about families working together. Draw lines and circles for the words you write.

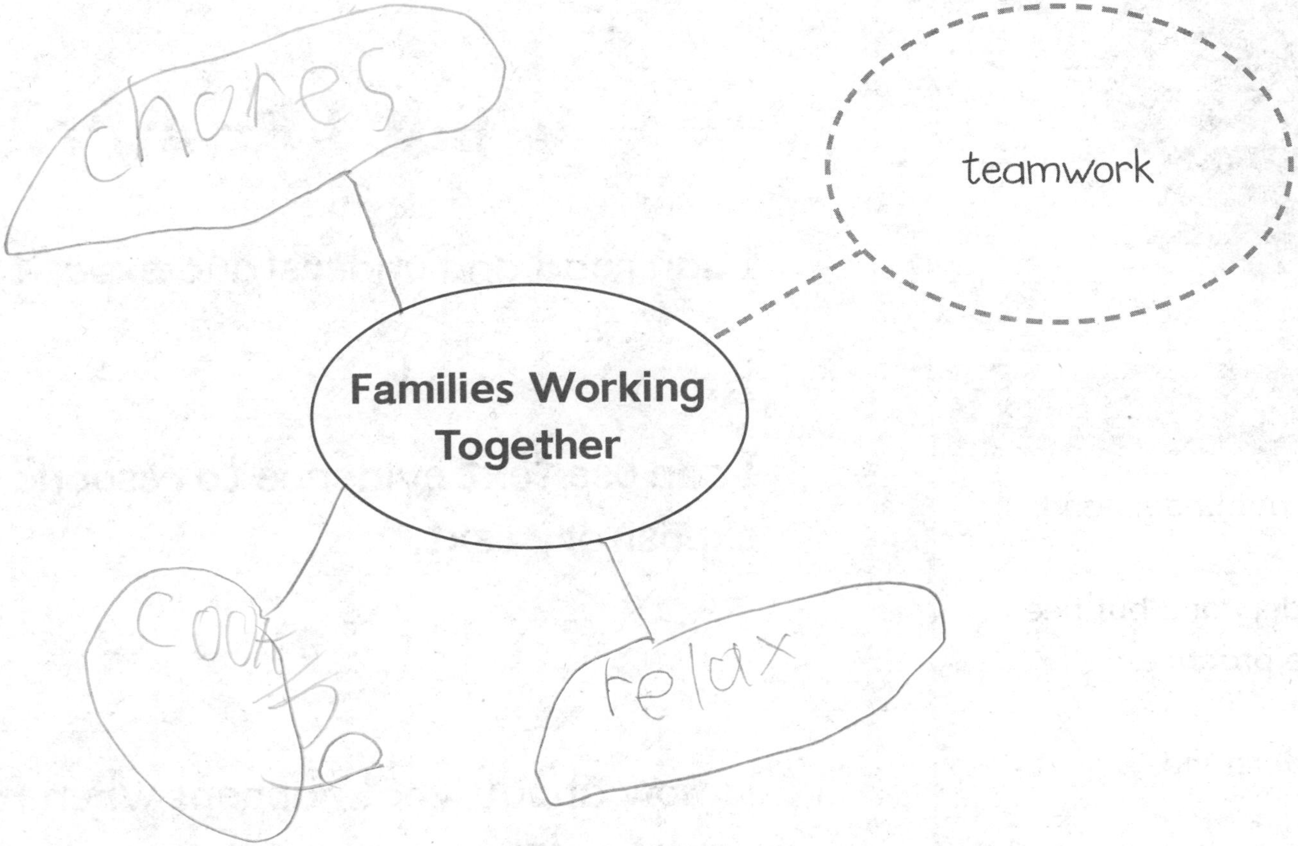

chores

teamwork

Families Working Together

cooking

relax

 Go online to **my.mheducation.com** and read the "A Job for Everyone" Blast. Think about how a family can start a business. Then blast back your response.

MY GOALS

Think about what you already know. Fill in the bars. You'll keep learning more.

What I Know Now

I can read and understand expository text.

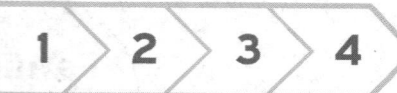

| 1 | 2 | 3 | 4 |

I can use text evidence to respond to expository text.

| 1 | 2 | 3 | 4 |

I know about what happens when families work together.

| 1 | 2 | 3 | 4 |

Key

1 =	I do not understand.
2 =	I understand but need more practice.
3 =	I understand.
4 =	I understand and can teach someone.

STOP You will come back to the next page later.

Think about what you learned. Fill in the bars. Keep up the good work!

What I Learned

I can read and understand expository text.

1 > 2 > 3 > 4

I can use text evidence to respond to expository text.

1 > 2 > 3 > 4

I know about what happens when families work together.

1 > 2 > 3 > 4

My Goal I can read and understand expository text.

TAKE NOTES

As you read, write down interesting words and important information.

_____

_____

_____

_____

_____

_____

_____

_____

Essential Question

?

What happens when families work together?

Read about how one family works to meet their needs.

Comstock/Stockbyte/Getty Images

Families Work!

Ellen Yung had a busy day at work! She put a cast on a broken arm, used a bandage to cover a deep cut, and helped twenty patients. Ellen is a doctor for children. **Customers** can get sick at any time, so pediatricians work long hours. They have hard **jobs**.

Ellen's husband works long hours, too. Steve is a firefighter. At the firehouse, he makes sure the **tools** work properly. He **checks** the hoses and fire trucks. At the fire, Steve rescues people from hot flames and smoke. The firefighters all work together to put out the fire.

When a fire alarm sounds, Steve suits up quickly.

PBNJ Productions/Blend Images

FIND TEXT EVIDENCE

Read

Paragraph 1
Topic and Details
Underline details that tell why Ellen had a busy day. Why do doctors like Ellen work long hours?

customers can get sick at any time

Paragraph 2
Synonyms
Circle *flames* in the text. Then **circle** a word with almost the same meaning.

Reread

Author's Craft

How does the author compare the jobs that Ellen and Steve have?

TIME for **KiDS**

FIND TEXT EVIDENCE

Read

Paragraph 1

Ask and Answer Questions
Ask a question about a way two family members work together.

_____

_____

Underline text evidence that helps you answer it.

Paragraph 2

Topic and Details
Circle details that tell why the family decides to buy a washing machine.

Reread
Author's Craft

How does the author use a photograph and caption to add information to the text?

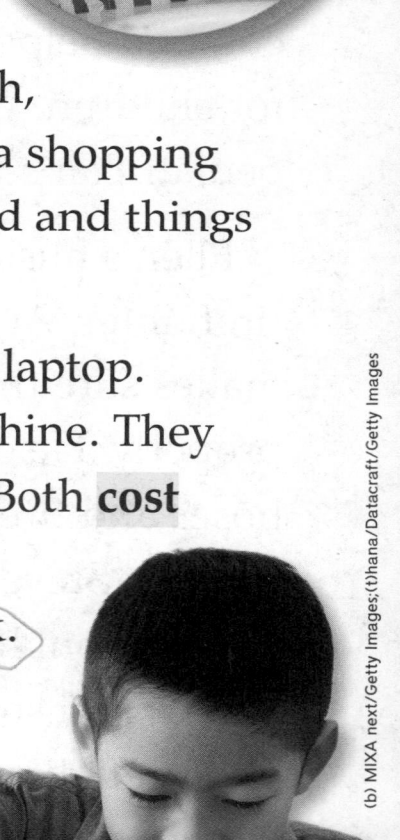

At home, the Yung family works together, too. Hanna sets the table for dinner. She also helps wash the dishes. Everyone has weekly **chores**. Mom and Hanna do the dusting and mopping. Dad and her brother, Zac, do the laundry. They wash, dry, and fold the clothes. Mom makes a shopping list each week. She lists items they need and things they want.

A short time ago, Zac wanted a new laptop. The family needed a new washing machine. They could only **spend** money on one item. Both **cost** the same. They had to **choose**. Clean clothes are needed for school and work. A new laptop is nice, but did Zac need it? Ellen and Steve thought about their family's needs. They decided to buy the washing machine.

Hanna's brother, Zac, helps with the meals.

(b) MIXA next/Getty Images;(t)hana/Datacraft/Getty Images

What Are Some Needs and Wants?

Needs	Wants
Water	Skateboard
Food	Video game
Shelter	Basketball
Clothing	

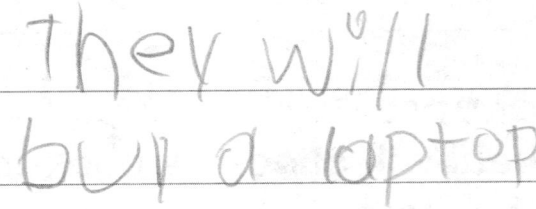

Zac knows that his parents have busy jobs. They bring home money to pay for their needs and wants. They needed that washing machine. Zac still wants a laptop. The family has decided to save some money each week so they can buy it in the future.

(l)©McGraw-Hill Education/Ken Karp; (r)C Squared Studios/Photodisc/Getty Images

Retell

Use your notes to help you retell the important facts and ideas in "Families Work!"

FIND TEXT EVIDENCE

Read

Chart

Draw a box around the title of the chart. **Circle** the heading of each column.

Paragraph 1
Topic and Details
What will the family buy in the future?

They will buy a laptop

Underline text evidence that explains how they will be able to buy it.

Reread
Author's Craft

Why does the author show the two photographs with the chart?

Vocabulary

Talk with a partner about each word. Then answer the questions.

checks

Mom **checks** the car tires before a trip.

Who checks the mailbox in your family?

_____

_____

choose

Raul will **choose** a book to read to the class.

What will you choose to read today?

_____

_____

Build Your Word List Draw a box around the word *save* on page 71. Use a word web to write more forms of the word in your reader's notebook. You may use a dictionary to help you.

chores

One of my **chores** is to feed our dog.

What is one of your chores?

_____

_____

cost

We bought a book that did not **cost** a lot of money.

What is a gift that doesn't cost a lot of money?

_____

_____

customers

Many **customers** visited the new store.

What can customers buy at a supermarket?

_____

_____

jobs

Nurse and doctor are two **jobs** at a hospital.

What are two jobs at a school?

_____

_____

spend

Greg decided to **spend** his money on a game.

What are two things families spend their money on?

_____

_____

tools

My mother used **tools** to fix my brother's bicycle.

What are tools you saw an adult use?

_____

Synonyms

Synonyms are words that have almost the same meaning. *Big* and *large* are synonyms.

🔍 FIND TEXT EVIDENCE

On page 70, I read Mom "lists items they need and things they want." In this sentence, items *and* things *are synonyms. I see that items are things on a list.*

She lists ⬚items⬚ they need and ⬚things⬚ they want.

Your Turn Use a print or digital thesaurus to write a synonym for the word below.

jobs, page 71 _____

CHECK IN ⟩ 1 ⟩ 2 ⟩ 3 ⟩ 4 ⟩

hana/Datacraft/Getty Images

Ask and Answer Questions

When you read, asking questions helps you think about parts of the text you may have missed or do not understand well.

FIND TEXT EVIDENCE

As I read the last paragraph on page 70, I ask myself, "Why did the family decide to buy a washing machine instead of a laptop?"

> Page 70
>
> A short time ago, Zac wanted a new laptop. The family needed a new washing machine. They could only spend money on one item. Both cost the same. They had to choose.

When I reread to answer my question, I understand the family could only buy one of the things. The family had to make a choice.

Your Turn Think of a question you have about the selection. Reread the parts of the text that will help you answer your question.

_____

_____

_____

Charts

"Families Work!" is an expository text. It gives facts and information about a topic. It can have text features, such as photographs with captions and charts.

🔍 FIND TEXT EVIDENCE

I can tell that "Families Work!" is expository text because it gives facts about how family members work to meet their needs. It also has text features.

When you write expository text, think about how to show information in a chart. Give your chart a title. Add headings that tell how the information is organized.

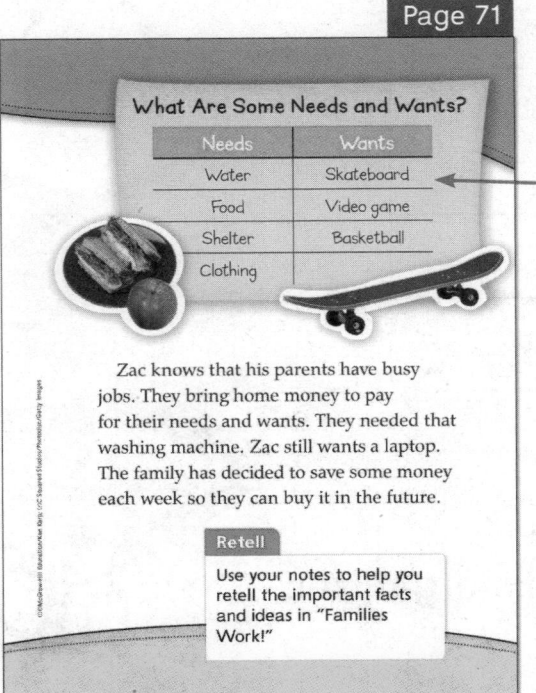

Page 71

What Are Some Needs and Wants?

Needs	Wants
Water	Skateboard
Food	Video game
Shelter	Basketball
Clothing	

Zac knows that his parents have busy jobs. They bring home money to pay for their needs and wants. They needed that washing machine. Zac still wants a laptop. The family has decided to save some money each week so they can buy it in the future.

Retell

Use your notes to help you retell the important facts and ideas in "Families Work!"

Chart

A chart shows information in an organized way that is easy to see. Facts may be in rows and columns.

Your Turn How does the chart help readers learn more about the topic?

_____

_____

_____

CHECK IN 1 2 3 4

Topic and Relevant Details

The topic is what the selection is about. A relevant detail is important information the author wants you to know about the topic.

🔍 **FIND TEXT EVIDENCE**

On page 69, I understand from the text and title that the selection is about the work that a family does. This must be the topic. I learn that Ellen Yung is a pediatrician, and Steve works as a firefighter.

Topic
The Yung Family's Work
Detail
Ellen is a pediatrician, and Steve is a firefighter.

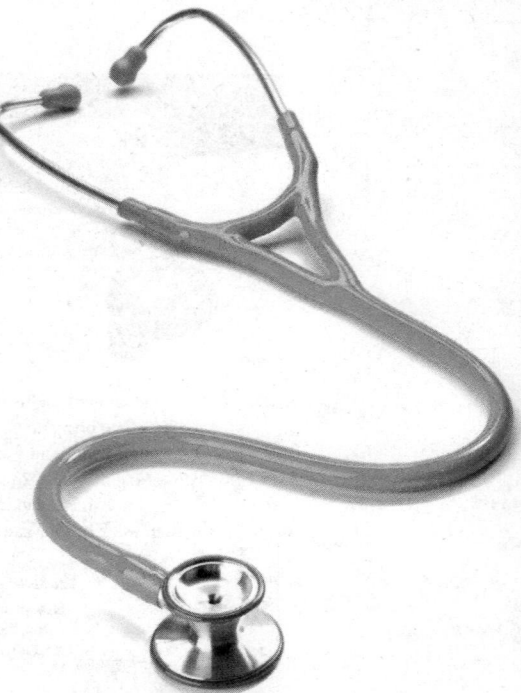

Your Turn Continue reading "Families Work!" Identify relevant details and fill in the graphic organizer.

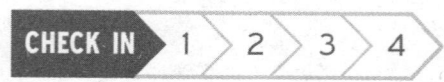

CHECK IN 1 2 3 4

matin/Shutterstock.com

Topic		
The Yung Family's Work		
Detail	**Detail**	**Detail**
Ellen is a pediatrician, and Steve is a firefighter.	They help each with chors.	They help each with the disis and londge clening.

PBNJ Productions/Blend Images

Respond to Reading

My Goal I can use text evidence to respond to expository text.

Talk about the prompt below. Use your notes and text evidence to support your response.

COLLABORATE

How does the Yung family decide how to spend their money?

_____

_____

_____

_____

_____

_____

_____

_____

Quick Tip

Use these sentence starters to help you organize your text evidence.

The family chooses to spend money on...

Then the family can...

For example...

Grammar Connections

When three or more items are listed, put a comma after each item.

For example:

They need water, food, shelter, and clothing.

CHECK IN 1 > 2 > 3 > 4 >

Interesting Jobs

With a partner, interview someone you know who has a job that interests you. Follow the research process to write a job description sheet.

Step 1 **Set a Goal** Choose a job that interests you.

Step 2 **Identify Sources** Prepare questions about the job for the interview.

_____

_____

_____

Step 3 **Find and Record Information** Take careful notes during the interview. Find or draw pictures that show important information from the responses.

Step 4 **Organize and Combine Information** List the ideas you want to include. Add details from your notes that tell about these ideas.

Step 5 **Create and Present** Write and illustrate your final job description sheet. Practice how to present it to the class.

Yunus Arakon/Hocus Focus Studio/E+/Getty Images

CHECK IN 1 2 3 4

Families Working Together

Literature Anthology: pages 60–63

? How does the author help you understand what Mary and her mom do on Tuesdays in the summer?

Talk About It Reread page 61. Why do you think the author begins the selection with the time?

Cite Text Evidence Answer the questions about the trip Mary and her mom make with details from the text.

Where do they go?	What do they do?	What does Mary say?

Write The author helps me understand what Mary and

her mom do on Tuesdays _____

_____

CHECK IN ⟩ 1 ⟩ 2 ⟩ 3 ⟩ 4 ⟩

? **How does the author use text features to help you understand who consumers are?**

Talk About It Look at the text features on pages 62 and 63. Talk about what the sidebar and photographs tell about consumers.

Cite Text Evidence Write three ways that text features help you understand who consumers are.

Sidebar Text	Chart	Photographs

Write The text features help me understand who

consumers are by _____

_____

_____

Quick Tip

Use the sentence starters to talk about the text.

The text in the sidebar explains...

The chart shows...

The photos and captions...

 Evaluate Information

How do the Gelders earn money with the fresh fruit they do not sell?

CHECK IN 1 2 3 4

Respond to Reading

COLLABORATE Discuss the prompt below. Use your notes and text evidence to support your answer.

Why is it important for the Gelders to work together?

_____

_____

_____

_____

_____

_____

_____

_____

_____

Quick Tip

Use these sentence starters to organize your text evidence.

Each day, the family...

Each person has...

The family can sell...

CHECK IN 1 > 2 > 3 > 4

Can Kids Help at Home?

Yes! Chores Are a Part of Growing Up

Doing chores not only helps adult family members, it benefits kids. It teaches them teamwork. Kids work with others to finish tasks. They learn the value of doing their part. Kids also gain confidence when they can help. In addition, doing chores is time families can spend together. Kids get even more than they give by doing their chores.

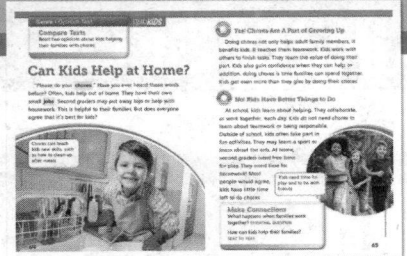

Literature Anthology pages 64–65

Reread the page. **Circle** what chores teach. **Underline** how kids learn this from chores.

Draw a box around why, or when, kids gain confidence.

What can families do as a result of chores?

_____

_____

_____

_____

COLLABORATE

Discuss why the author reminds readers of the opinion at the end. Use vocabulary from the selection.

Sergey Novikov/Shutterstock

No! Kids Have Better Things to Do

At school, kids learn about helping. They collaborate, or work together, each day. Kids do not need chores to learn about teamwork or being responsible. Outside of school, kids often take part in fun activities. They may learn a sport or learn about the arts. At home, second graders need free time for play. They need time for homework! Most people would agree, kids have little time left to do chores.

Reread the page. **Underline** why the author believes kids don't need chores to learn about teamwork or being responsible.

What is another reason the author believes the opinion in the text?

_____

_____

_____

_____

_____

COLLABORATE

Discuss the evidence that supports why kids should not do chores. Use vocabulary from the selection.

CHECK IN 1 2 3 4

monkeybusinessimages/iStock/Getty Images

Author's Opinion

An author's opinion is something the author believes is true. Authors use facts and other details, or evidence, to show readers why they believe the opinion is true.

FIND TEXT EVIDENCE

Reread the text on page 83. The author believes that kids should do chores for the benefits they get.

> Doing chores not only helps adult family members, it benefits kids.

What are two examples of the benefits kids get from doing chores?

_____

_____

Your Turn Reread the text on page 84. What evidence supports why kids have little time to do chores?

COLLABORATE

_____

_____

CHECK IN 1 2 3 4

MAKE CONNECTIONS

? **What have you learned from the selections and the photograph about families working together?**

Talk About It Look at the photograph and read the caption. Talk with a partner about what the family members are doing.

COLLABORATE

Cite Text Evidence **Circle** details in the photo and caption that show how the family feels when they do work together.

Write The selections I read and this photograph help me understand how families

_____

_____

_____

_____

_____

_____

Quick Tip

Describe what you see in the photograph. Use these sentence starters.

The family is...

Each family member is...

The family looks...

This family enjoys washing the car on a sunny day.

CHECK IN 1 2 3 4

My Goal I know about what happens when families work together.

Write an Essay

Think about the families you read about. The family members all worked together. What are the benefits of working together as a family?

1. Look at your Build Knowledge notes in your reader's notebook.

2. Write an essay that explains the reasons family members should work together. Use examples from three of the texts you read.

3. Include some of the new words you learned. Remember to use evidence from the texts to support your ideas.

Think about what you learned in this text set. Fill in the bars on page 67.

Think about what you already know. Fill in the bars. Meeting your goals may take time.

Key

1 = I do not understand.

2 = I understand but need more practice.

3 = I understand.

4 = I understand and can teach someone.

What I Know Now

I can write realistic fiction.

| 1 | 2 | 3 | 4 |

I can write an expository essay.

| 1 | 2 | 3 | 4 |

STOP You will come back to the next page later.

Think about what you learned. Fill in the bars. What do you want to work on more?

What I Learned

I can write realistic fiction.

1 > 2 > 3 > 4

I can write an expository essay.

1 > 2 > 3 > 4

My Goal

I can write realistic fiction.

Expert Model

Features of Realistic Fiction

Realistic fiction is a story that could happen in real life.

- The characters act and speak like real people.

- The narrator uses words that tell sequence, or the order of events.

- The story has a beginning, middle, and end.

Literature Anthology: pages 10–31

Analyze an Expert Model Studying *Big Red Lollipop* will help you learn how to write realistic fiction. Reread page 25. Answer the questions below.

How do you know that time has gone by in the story?

The author uses the words "then one day"!.

How does the author show that Sana has a problem?

The author uses exclamation points to show Sana is yelling!

Plan: Brainstorm

Generate Ideas You will write realistic fiction about a family. Use this space for your ideas. Draw and brainstorm words that describe the characters, setting, and events you might write about.

CHECK IN   1   2   3   4

Plan: Choose Your Topic

Writing Prompt Write realistic fiction about a character in a family. Show how the character's feelings change. Complete these sentences to get started.

My characters are _boy bad gilr_

At the beginning of the story, _the boy wos sard adjnot to go_

In the middle, _he badand sistr wos cering him on_

At the end, _he jumped into the pool._

Purpose and Audience Some authors write realistic fiction to entertain their audience. They may also want to show how people learn and grow. Think about why you chose your characters. Then explain the purpose for writing your story in your writer's notebook.

CHECK IN ▷ 1 ▷ 2 ▷ 3 ▷ 4

Plan: Organization

Develop Sequence Authors think about the order, or sequence, of events in a story. Read the chart below. Write *first*, *next*, and *last* to show the sequence of events.

Quick Tip

Some words and phrases help show that the story is moving from one part to the next. You can use words like *first, later, then, after that, when, finally,* and *in the end.*

_____, the backyard gate is open. Annie's puppy is gone!

⬇

_____, Mom and Dad help look for Daisy. They hear a bark.

⬇

_____, they see Annie's friend Gina. She is holding the puppy! "Daisy wanted to visit my yard," Gina laughs.

Plan In your writer's notebook, make a chart like the one above. Fill it in with details about what happens at the beginning, middle, and end of your story.

CHECK IN 1 ❯ 2 ❯ 3 ❯ 4

Draft

Descriptive Details The author of "Maria Celebrates Brazil" uses details to describe the characters and setting in the beginning of the story.

> Maria and her family are in their bright, hot kitchen. "Please, Mãe, por favor!" Maria begs.
>
> Mãe speaks Portuguese. This is the language of Brazil. "No matter how much you beg or plead, you must go to practice. The parade is next week."

Use the paragraphs as a model to start writing. Think about details that describe your setting. Include descriptive details in the words your characters speak.

_____

_____

_____

Write a Draft Look over the chart you made. Use it to help you write your draft in your notebook. Remember to use details that describe, or tell about, your characters, settings, and events.

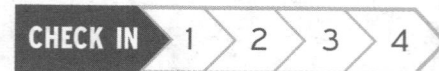
CHECK IN 1 2 3 4

Revise

Strong Openings A strong opening grabs your attention and makes you want to find out what happens next. Read the story opening below. Then revise it. Add details about the character and his problem to make readers interested in the story.

Quick Tip

Strong openings can describe a problem a character faces, or has, in the story. Think about details that show what the character feels about the problem. Dialogue, or what a character says, can show strong feelings.

> Tim had slept late. He needed to make a picnic for Father's Day.
>
> Outside his bedroom window, there were clouds.

_____

_____

_____

_____

_____

Revise It's time to revise your draft. Include a strong opening that makes your reader want to find out what happens next.

CHECK IN 1 2 3 4

Revise: Peer Conferences

COLLABORATE

Review a Draft Listen carefully as a partner reads his or her work aloud. Begin by telling what you liked about the draft. Ask questions and make suggestions that give the writer ideas for making the writing stronger.

Partner Feedback Write one suggestion that you will use in the revision of your story.

Based on my partner's feedback, I will _____

_____

_____

After you finish giving each other feedback, reflect on the peer conference. What was helpful? What might you do differently next time?

_____

_____

Revision Use the Revising Checklist to help you figure out what text you may need to move, add to, or delete. Remember to use the rubric on page 99 to help you with your revision.

Remember to use the rubric on page 99

Quick Tip

Use these sentence starters to discuss your partner's work.

I enjoyed your story opening because…

How about adding details about…

I have a question about…

✔ Revising Checklist

- ☐ Does my story fit my purpose and audience?
- ☐ Does it include descriptive details?
- ☐ Does it have a strong opening?
- ☐ Does the story have a beginning, middle, and end?

Edit and Proofread

When you **edit** and **proofread**, you look for and correct mistakes in your writing. Rereading a revised draft several times will help you catch any errors. Use the checklist below to edit your sentences.

Grammar Connections

When you revise your writing, make sure that you capitalize the first word in every sentence. Be sure to use the correct end punctuation for all of your sentences.

✓ Editing Checklist

☐ Are all sentences complete sentences?

☐ Do all questions end with question marks?

☐ Do sentences that show strong feelings, such as excitement, end with exclamation marks?

☐ Do statements end with periods?

☐ Are all the words spelled correctly?

List two mistakes you found as you proofread your story.

1 _____

_____

2 _____

_____

Publish, Present, and Evaluate

Publishing Create a clean, neat final copy of your story. You may add illustrations or other visuals to make your published work more interesting.

Presentation Practice your presentation when you are ready to present your work. Use the Presenting Checklist to help you.

Evaluate After you publish and present your story, use the rubric on the next page to evaluate your writing.

1 What did you do successfully? _____

_____

_____

_____

2 What needs more work? _____

_____

_____

_____

✔ Presenting Checklist

- ☐ Sit up or stand up straight.
- ☐ Look at the audience.
- ☐ Speak slowly and clearly.
- ☐ Speak loud enough so that everyone can hear you.
- ☐ Answer questions using details from your story.

4	3	2	1
• tells a lively, descriptive realistic fiction story about a character in a family • begins with a strong, detailed opening • has a clear beginning, middle, and end • is free or almost free of errors	• tells a somewhat descriptive story about a character in a family • begins with a strong opening • has a beginning, middle, and end • has few errors	• tries to write realistic fiction but details are unclear • lacks a strong opening • makes an effort to sequence events and create a beginning, middle, and end • has many errors that distract from the meaning of the story	• does not focus writing on the genre or topic • lacks an opening • does not sequence events into a beginning, middle, and end • has many errors that make the story hard to understand

Turn to page 89. Fill in the bars to show what you learned.

My Goal

I can write an expository essay.

Expert Model

Features of an Expository Essay

An expository essay is a kind of expository text.

- It gives facts about the topic.

- It has a concluding statement or section.

Literature Anthology: pages 60–63

Analyze an Expert Model Studying "Families Working Together" will help you learn to write an expository essay. Reread page 61. Answer the questions below.

Why does the author begin the text with a question?

The question tells
us the topic of the story.

How does the author show the way Mary feels about selling the food her family grows?

He uses mary's words
to show us how she
feels.

Word Wise

The author uses the names of family members. The names help readers understand what each person does and how the members of the family work together.

Plan: Brainstorm

Generate Ideas You will write an **expository essay** about a person who works for the community. Use this space for your ideas. Brainstorm ideas about community workers who interest you. Write or draw your ideas.

Quick Tip

Think about the people that you see working in your community. Choose people with jobs that are helpful to others.

they the nes is hpel
npel the pushyto
peoplo. the

STOP

They tel the prsi whut to be.

CHECK IN 1 2 3 4

Plan: Choose Your Topic

Writing Prompt Write an expository essay that explains what a community worker does. Complete these sentences to help you get started.

My community worker is _____ nurse _____

I think this job is important because _____ They save people. _____

I will get information about this worker by _____ research _____

Purpose and Audience Authors may write to teach others about their communities. Think about why you chose your topic. Then explain your purpose for writing in your writer's notebook.

Digital Tools

To learn about how to identify your purpose and audience, watch "Purpose of Informative Writing." Go to **my.mheducation.com**.

George Doyle/age fotostock

CHECK IN 1 2 3 4

Plan: Research

Develop Questions Authors may write questions they want to answer in an expository essay. Read an author's questions in the web below. Write two more questions about being a firefighter.

What equipment do you need at work?

What tasks do you do every day?

Firefighter

 **Plan** In your writer's notebook, make a web like the one above for your topic. Write questions that you will answer in your essay.

Draft

COLLABORATE

Sentence Types and Lengths
Writers use long and short sentences to make their writing interesting and easy to read. They also use different types of sentences to add interest.

- A **statement** gives information.

- A **question** asks something.

- An **exclamation** shows strong feelings.

Read the paragraph below. **Circle** the question and **draw a box** around the exclamation. **Underline** the longer sentences.

> The family gets up early, and they work for many hours. What foods do they sell? They sell fruits and vegetables. The foods are so delicious! One popular food is strawberries, so the family plants a lot of them.

Write a Draft Use information you gathered to write a draft. Include different types of sentences. Try to use both short and longer sentences in your draft.

Grammar Connections

You can combine two sentences by joining two nouns in the subject or predicate with the conjunction *and*.

Mr. Ryan is a librarian. Mrs. Garcia is a librarian.
Mr. Ryan and Mrs. Garcia are librarians.

CHECK IN 1 2 3 4

Revise

Details Authors add details, such as facts, to help readers understand ideas. Read the text below about Steve Yung's work as a firefighter. Revise the text with details from page 69 that tell more about his work.

> Steve is a firefighter. He works at the firehouse. His job is to
>
> rescue people and put out fires.

_____

_____

_____

_____

 **Revise** It's time to revise your draft. Make sure to include details that help readers understand what the person does and why this work is important to the community.

Revise: Peer Conferences

Review a Draft Listen carefully as a partner reads his or her work aloud. Begin by telling what you like about the draft. Make suggestions that you think will make the writing stronger.

Partner Feedback Write one of your partner's suggestions that you will use in the revision of your text.

Based on my partner's feedback, I will _____

_____

_____

After you finish giving each other feedback, reflect on the peer conference. What was helpful? What might you do differently next time?

_____

_____

Revision Use the Revising Checklist to help you figure out what text you may need to move, add to, or delete. Remember to use the rubric on page 109 to help you with your revision.

Quick Tip

Use these sentence starters to discuss your partner's work.

The details in your draft helped me understand...

How about adding more information about...

Can you tell me how...

Revising Checklist

- ☐ Does my essay give facts about the community worker?
- ☐ Does it answer my questions about the community worker?
- ☐ Do I make a concluding statement?
- ☐ Are there different sentence types and lengths?

Edit and Proofread

When you **edit** and **proofread**, you look for and correct mistakes in your writing. Rereading a revised draft several times will help you catch any errors. Use the checklist below to edit your sentences.

Tech Tip

If you type your essay, remember to use the "Tab" key to indent the first word of each paragraph.

✔ Editing Checklist

- ☐ Do all sentences begin with a capital letter and end with a punctuation mark?
- ☐ Are all the words spelled correctly?
- ☐ Are commas used correctly?
- ☐ Are all sentences complete sentences?
- ☐ Is the conjunction *and* used correctly to combine sentences?

Grammar Connections

Make sure you used commas to separate three or more items in a series.

I used the colors red, white, and blue in my poster.

List two mistakes you found as you proofread your text.

1 _____

_____

2 _____

_____

Publish, Present, and Evaluate

Publishing Create a neat, clean final copy of your expository essay. As you write your draft, be sure to print neatly and legibly. You may add illustrations or other visuals to make your published work more interesting.

Presentation Practice your presentation when you are ready to present your work. Use the Presenting Checklist to help you.

Evaluate After you publish and present your expository essay, use the rubric on the next page to evaluate your writing.

✓ Presenting Checklist

☐ Sit up or stand up straight.

☐ Look at different people in the audience.

☐ Speak slowly and clearly.

☐ Speak loudly so that everyone can hear you.

☐ Answer questions using facts from your essay.

1 What did you do successfully? _____

_____

_____

2 What needs more work? _____

_____

_____

4	3	2	1
• uses specific facts about a community worker's job • sentences vary in length and type • has a clear statement or paragraph that concludes the essay • is free or almost free of errors	• tells information about a community worker's job • sentences are different lengths • has a concluding statement • has few errors	• uses information that does not relate to the topic • sentences are mostly the same length • does not have a clear conclusion • has many errors that distract from the meaning of the essay	• most information is not based on facts from sources • sentence length is the same • does not have a concluding statement • has many errors that make the essay hard to understand

Turn to page 89. Fill in the bars to show what you learned.

My Goal I can read and understand social studies texts.

TAKE NOTES

Take notes and annotate as you read the passages "Community Heroes" and "Dad for Mayor!"

Look for the answer to the question: *How can people help their communities?*

PASSAGE 1

EXPOSITORY TEXT

COMMUNITY HEROES

Many firefighters do not get paid for their work. They are volunteers. They may work at other jobs to make money. Their work as firefighters is a gift to their community.

Volunteer firefighters work hard to keep the towns safe. They go through many hours of training. They get called to help people at all hours of the day and night.

Volunteers face the same dangers other firefighters face. They do more than just put out fires. They help at car crashes. They save people caught in floodwaters. They hurry to help people who become sick or hurt at home.

LAMB/Alamy Stock Photo

TAKE NOTES

These special helpers are part of a team. One person drives the truck. Others put up the ladder. Some hold the hose that sprays water on a fire. They help each other stay safe. The teams are like families. Some stations even have dogs.

Volunteer firefighters like helping their neighbors. The community helps them, too. People give money for trucks and tools. They take food to the firehouse. They thank firefighters for their important work. In this way, firefighters and community members work together to keep communities safe.

Volunteers Help Communities	Communities Help Volunteers
put out fires	give money for trucks and tools
after car crashes	take food to the firehouse
during floods	thank firefighters for their work

TAKE NOTES

_____

_____

_____

_____

_____

_____

_____

_____

_____

_____

_____

_____

_____

_____

PASSAGE 2 · **REALISTIC FICTION**

Dad for Mayor!

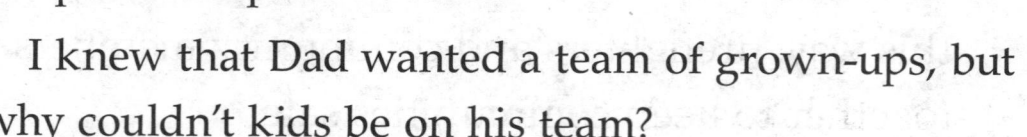

Dad likes helping our community. He talks to people in our town and hears ideas for making the town a better place. He has good ideas, too. He decided to run for mayor!

"I'll need a strong team," he told Mom. "I need help writing speeches. We need posters and people to telephone voters."

I knew that Dad wanted a team of grown-ups, but why couldn't kids be on his team?

At school, we are learning about elections. Our teacher said, "Voting is a way to make your voice heard." She said voters must understand the key issues and how government works. Some issues in our town are repairing the downtown bridge and making bike lanes. We also need a new library.

My friends and I met after school. We talked about improving our town. We sketched ideas for posters and listed reasons to vote for my dad. I think the best reason is that he listens to people and wants to make the town a better place for everyone. We also listed reasons why people should join his team.

I showed Mom and Dad our ideas. "Even if we can't vote," I said, "we can still have a voice." They were amazed. Dad said, "How thoughtless of me not to include you to help with the election!"

Thirty people worked on Dad's team. We learned a lot about elections. Can you guess the best part? Dad won, thanks to his great team!

TAKE NOTES

Compare the Passages

Talk About It Reread your notes from "Community Heroes" and "Dad for Mayor!" Talk with a partner about what you learned about firefighters and mayors.

Cite Text Evidence Fill in the chart with details from the texts that show how firefighters and mayors help their communities.

Firefighters	Mayors
1. They can be eney age. 2. they wrok hard to be a firerighter.	1. they nede a teme. 2. The mayors hav to wart a kup bay to now if they are the mayors

? **How can people help their communities?**

COLLABORATE

Talk About It Look at the graphic organizer on page 114. Talk about how firefighters and mayors help communities. Explain how their work is similar.

Write Firefighters and mayors both work to help

_____

_____

_____

_____

_____

Quick Tip

Use these sentence starters to describe how the work of firefighters and mayors is similar.

Firefighters and mayors both...

Firefighters help people during...

A mayor works to improve...

Combine Information

Think about what firefighters and mayors do. How do you know when to call a firefighter for help? What can you do to get the mayor of your town help make something better?

CHECK IN   1   2   3   4

Helping Your School Community

People help their communities in many ways. Talk with a partner about how you and your class can help your school community. Write and draw your ideas in the box.

Choose one idea with your partner. Draw a picture and write a caption to show your idea. Then share it with the class. Listen to other groups share their ideas.

Letter to the Principal

COLLABORATE

Think about the different ideas the class had for helping the school community. Talk with a partner about the ideas you liked best. Choose one that you would like to do. Write it here:

_____

Write a letter to your principal explaining the idea. Tell what you want to do and explain how it will help the school community.

Use these parts in your letter:

Heading: Write the date at the top.

Greeting: Begin with the word *Dear*, then your principal's name.

Body: Explain your idea.

Closing: Use a closing word or phrase, such as *Sincerely*. Then write your signature.

Quick Tip

- Write the heading at the top of your letter.
- Write the closing at the bottom of your letter.
- Always include commas after the greeting and the closing.

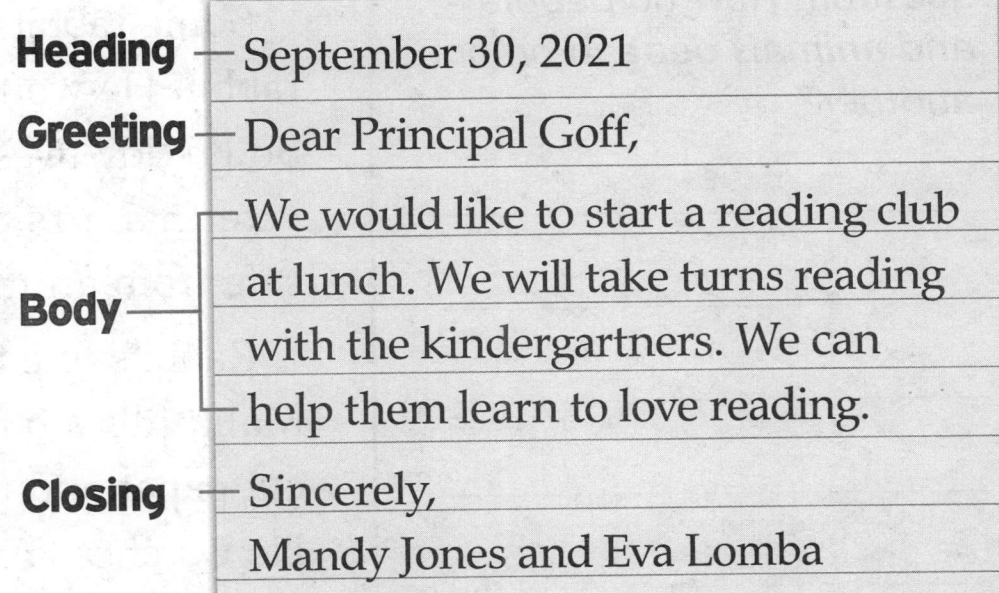

Heading — September 30, 2021

Greeting — Dear Principal Goff,

Body — We would like to start a reading club at lunch. We will take turns reading with the kindergartners. We can help them learn to love reading.

Closing — Sincerely,
Mandy Jones and Eva Lomba

My Goal I can read and understand science texts.

TAKE NOTES

Take notes and annotate as you read the passages "Taking Care of Freddy" and "Busy Bees."

Look for the answer to the question: *How do people and animals depend on one another?*

_____

_____

_____

_____

_____

PASSAGE **1** EXPOSITORY TEXT

Taking Care of Freddy

Malik's mom is a veterinarian. She is a doctor who takes care of animals. Sometimes she helps animals find new homes. Malik helps take care of the animals while they wait for a new family. This summer, he is taking care of Freddy the rabbit.

Some rabbits live in nature. But Freddy is a pet rabbit. He would not be able to survive outside. So Freddy lives in a big cage indoors at the veterinarian's office. He stays inside to keep safe from animals and other dangers.

Rabbits like to dig and chew. Malik fills a box halfway with cut paper and puts it in the cage. He watches Freddy dig in the box. Freddy even chews on the box!

TAKE NOTES

A rabbit needs exercise. Freddy is allowed to go outside when someone is with him. Malik watches Freddy as he hops around. A fence keeps the rabbit safe. Freddy rolls a ball around. Malik likes to play ball with Freddy.

Freddy needs care to be healthy. Malik's mom shows him how to brush Freddy's fur. This keeps Freddy's fur clean and healthy. Malik fills bowls with hay and rabbit food. He makes sure Freddy's water bowl is full. Rabbits drink lots of water.

Malik likes learning how to care for a rabbit. He really likes to play with Freddy. He hopes Freddy finds a new family soon.

TAKE NOTES

_____

_____

_____

_____

_____

_____

_____

_____

_____

_____

_____

_____

_____

PASSAGE 2   EXPOSITORY TEXT

BUSY BEES

Ana Ramirez has always loved honey. Her grandmother has more than a dozen beehives. A hive is where bees live. Ana helps her grandmother collect honey from the hives.

Honeybees work hard to make honey. They can visit up to 100 flowers on each trip! They collect nectar from flowers. They keep the nectar in their mouth, where it mixes with a special liquid. They store the nectar mixture at the hive. It then turns into honey. The bees put a layer of wax over the honey. They use the honey for food in winter.

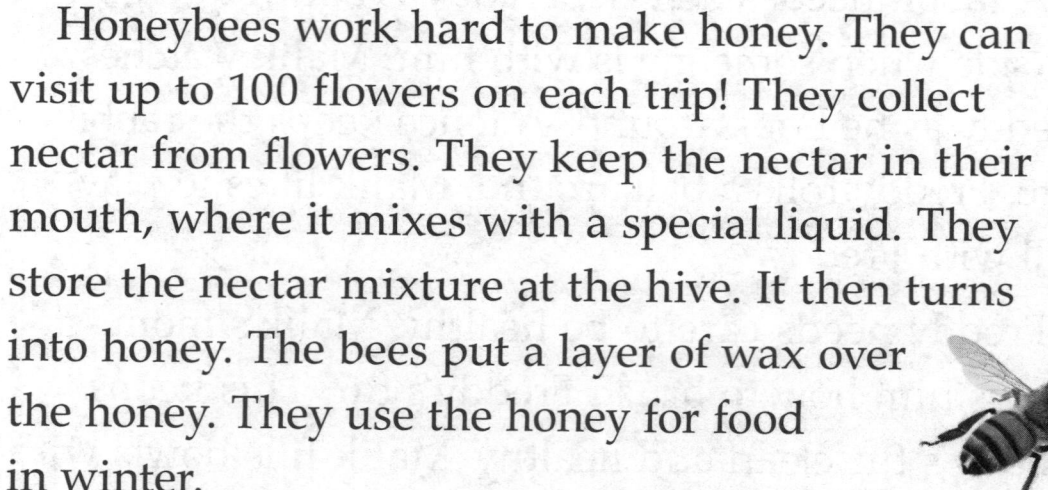

To collect the honey, Ana and her grandmother put on special clothes. These clothes protect them from the bees. They visit each hive and carefully move the bees away.

Next, Mrs. Ramirez takes square frames out of the hive. The frames are full of honey. They always leave enough honey for the bees to eat.

Ana helps her grandmother take the honey off the frames. First, they take off the wax. Then they put the frames in a machine. The machine spins the frames. The honey comes off the frames. Finally, Ana and her grandmother pour the honey into clean, glass jars.

They have more honey than their family can use. Ana's family sells the honey in their store. People for miles around enjoy Ana's honey.

Mrs. Ramirez and Ana collect honey from their beehives.

(b) Beth Rooney/Getty Images

TAKE NOTES

Compare the Passages

COLLABORATE

Talk About It Reread your notes from "Taking Care of Freddy" and "Busy Bees." Talk with a partner about what the people and animals do in each passage.

Cite Text Evidence Fill in the chart with details that describe what the people and animals do.

"Taking Care of Freddy"	"Busy Bees"
Malik	Ana and her grandmother
Freddy	Bees

?How do people and animals depend on one another?

Talk About It Look at the graphic organizer on page 122. Talk about "Taking Care of Freddy" and "Busy Bees." What does each person and animal need? How do they help one another meet their needs?

Write Animals need _____

_____

_____

People need _____

_____

_____

Quick Tip

Use these sentence starters to discuss how people and animals can help each other meet their needs.

Rabbits need...

Malik can...

Ana and her grandmother...

The bees need...

💡 Combine Information

Why is it important for people to think about the needs of animals?

CHECK IN 1 > 2 > 3 > 4

Write a Pet Owner Book

Write a book to help people take care of their cat, dog, rabbit, or other pet. Find out what the animal needs. Give information about how people can help meet those needs. Use these tips:

- Tell what the pet should eat and drink.

- Give examples of toys that the pet would like.

- Share information about grooming (baths, brushing teeth, clipping nails).

- Include information about when a pet should go to the veterinarian.

To help you get started, draw a picture and name the pet you are choosing for your book below.

Quick Tip

You can use a chart to help you organize the information in your book. Write the headings *Feeding*, *Playing*, *Grooming*, and *Health*. Include the most important information about what the pet needs.

Reflect on Your Learning

 **Talk About It** Reflect on what you learned in this unit. Then talk with a partner about how you did.

I am really proud of how I can _____

_____

_____

_____

Something I need to work more on is _____

_____

_____

_____

Share a goal you have with a partner.

 **My Goal** Set a goal for Unit 2. In your reader's notebook, write about what you can do to get there.